CGP hatches a Handwriting plan for spring!

It's crucial to keep working on Handwriting skills throughout Year 3, and this CGP book is a brilliant way to keep pupils practising regularly...

It's packed with fun, engaging exercises for every day of spring term, covering all the words they'll need to use most often.

We've included plenty of full sentences and longer pieces to tackle too — perfect for helping them build up their fluency and confidence!

What CGP is all about

Our sole aim here at CGP is to produce the highest quality books — carefully written, immaculately presented and dangerously close to being funny.

Then we work our socks off to get them out to you — at the cheapest possible prices.

Contents

☑ Use the tick boxes to help keep a record of which pages have been attempted.

Week 1
- ☑ Day 1 1
- ☑ Day 2 2
- ☑ Day 3 3
- ☑ Day 4 4
- ☑ Day 5 5

Week 2
- ☑ Day 1 6
- ☑ Day 2 7
- ☑ Day 3 8
- ☑ Day 4 9
- ☑ Day 5 10

Week 3
- ☑ Day 1 11
- ☑ Day 2 12
- ☑ Day 3 13
- ☑ Day 4 14
- ☑ Day 5 15

Week 4
- ☑ Day 1 16
- ☑ Day 2 17
- ☑ Day 3 18
- ☑ Day 4 19
- ☑ Day 5 20

Week 5
- ☑ Day 1 21
- ☑ Day 2 22
- ☑ Day 3 23
- ☑ Day 4 24
- ☑ Day 5 25

Week 6
- ☑ Day 1 26
- ☑ Day 2 27
- ☑ Day 3 28
- ☑ Day 4 29
- ☑ Day 5 30

Week 7
- ☑ Day 1 31
- ☑ Day 2 32
- ☑ Day 3 33
- ☑ Day 4 34
- ☑ Day 5 35

Week 8
- ☑ Day 1 36
- ☑ Day 2 37
- ☑ Day 3 38
- ☑ Day 4 39
- ☑ Day 5 40

Week 9

- [ ] Day 1 41
- [ ] Day 2 42
- [ ] Day 3 43
- [ ] Day 4 44
- [ ] Day 5 45

Week 10

- [ ] Day 1 46
- [ ] Day 2 47
- [ ] Day 3 48
- [ ] Day 4 49
- [ ] Day 5 50

Week 11

- [ ] Day 1 51
- [ ] Day 2 52
- [ ] Day 3 53
- [ ] Day 4 54
- [ ] Day 5 55

Week 12

- [ ] Day 1 56
- [ ] Day 2 57
- [ ] Day 3 58
- [ ] Day 4 59
- [ ] Day 5 60

Published by CGP

ISBN: 978 1 78908 662 1

Editors: Luke Bennett, Ellen Burton, Eleanor Crabtree and Hayley Thompson.

With thanks to Sharon Keeley-Holden and Lucy Towle for the proofreading.
With thanks to Emily Smith for the copyright research.

Printed by Elanders Ltd, Newcastle upon Tyne.
Clipart on the cover and throughout the book from Corel®
Images used on page 60 © www.edu-clips.com
Based on the classic CGP style created by Richard Parsons.

Text, design, layout and original illustrations © Coordination Group Publications Ltd. (CGP) 2020
All rights reserved.

Photocopying this book is not permitted, even if you have a CLA licence.
Extra copies are available from CGP with next day delivery • 0800 1712 712 • www.cgpbooks.co.uk

How to Use this Book

- This book contains 60 pages of daily handwriting practice.

- It's split into 12 sections — that's roughly one section for each week of the Year 3 Spring term.

- A week is made up of 5 pages, so there's one for every school day of the term (Monday – Friday).

- Each page should take about 10 minutes to complete.

- Pupils practise copying individual words, including spelling list words from the National Curriculum, and whole sentences. This helps them to build up their handwriting fluency. Towards the end of the book, they are also given some whole paragraphs to copy.

- Typical pages look something like this:

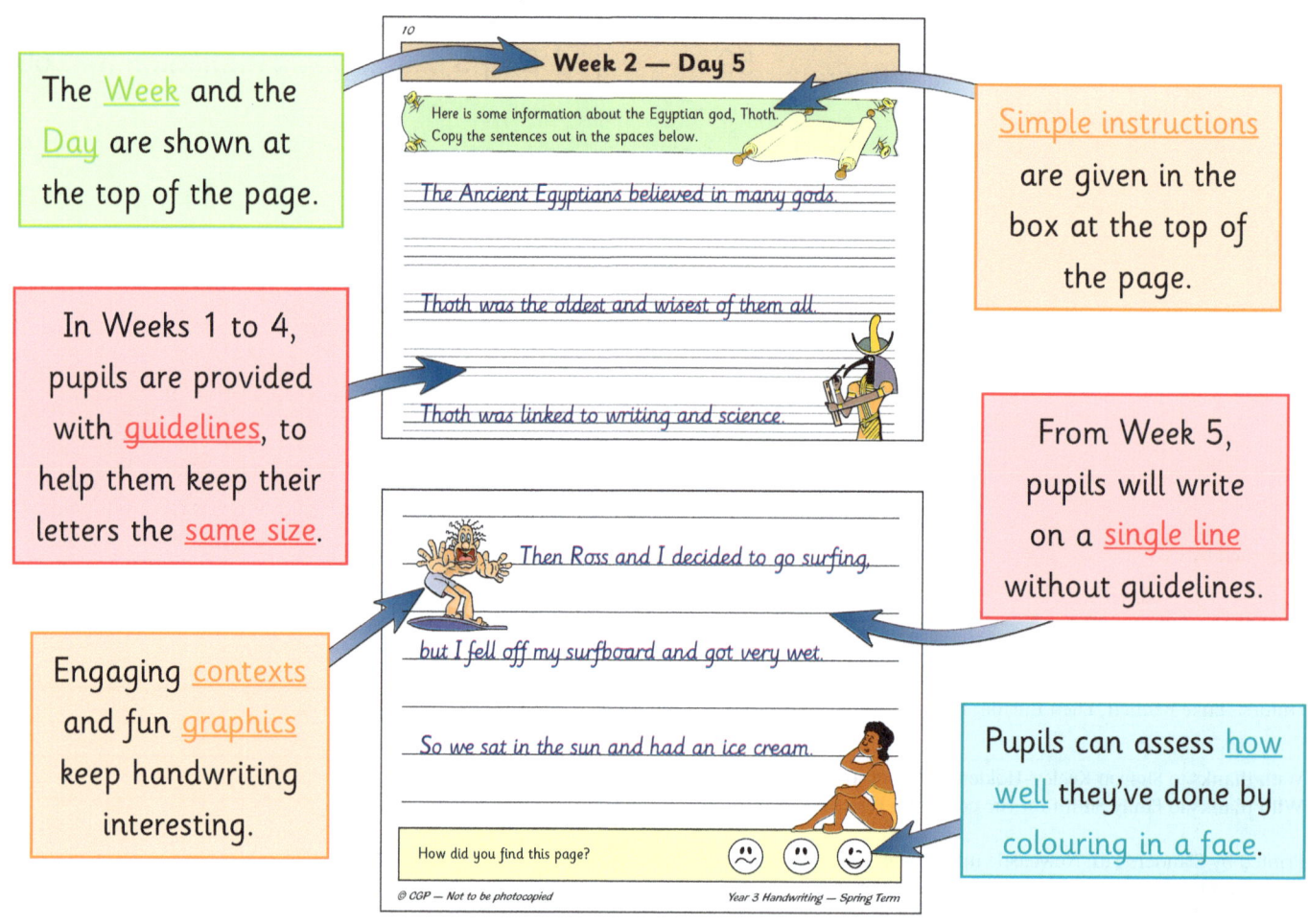

If you are a parent or guardian using this book at home with your child, you should bear in mind that different schools have different handwriting styles. You should check with the school to see how they write and join each letter. Some schools also have different break letters (letters that don't join to the next letter). For example, 'g' can be a break letter or can be joined. You should check which break letters the school uses.

Week 1 — Day 1

Here are ten common letter pairs, and five words containing some of these letter pairs. Copy everything out twice, as neatly as you can.

th   as

er   to

es   ng

an   ha

in   nd

mother

   branches

stopping

cashier

handstand

How did you get on with this page?

Week 1 — Day 2

There are ten common letter pairs written below, and five words containing some of these letter pairs. Copy all of them out twice.

he

at

en

ed

ve

ou

le

it

or

on

baton

brittle

rounded

 heavenly

chores

How did you find doing this page?

Week 1 — Day 3

Here are the names of ten countries in Europe. Copy each one out once. Remember to make your capital letters touch the top line.

England

Scotland

Northern Ireland

Wales

France

Iceland

Spain

Germany

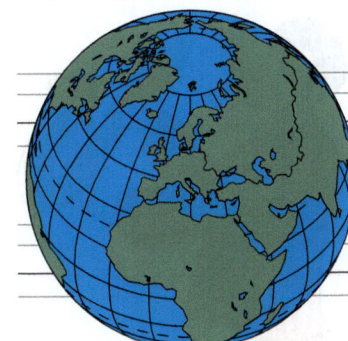
Denmark

Poland

How did you get on with writing these countries?

Week 1 — Day 4

Here are five sentences for you to copy out.
They all mention a month or day of the week.

They are getting married in September.

On Tuesday, we went on a school trip.

My party is on Saturday the 21st of July.

Spring begins in March and ends in June.

I play in a jazz band every Thursday.

How neatly did you write these sentences?

Week 1 — Day 5

A contraction is when two words are joined together, with an apostrophe showing where letters have been missed out.
Copy out these sentences, which all contain contractions.

I'm looking forward to a holiday.

He hasn't been behaving himself at school.

They'd like some chocolate biscuits.

I wish I didn't have to do this homework.

She couldn't reach the highest shelf.

How well did these sentences go?

Week 2 — Day 1

Here is a list of ten words. Copy each one out three times.

woman

women

recent

history

guard

certain

circle

early

position

separate

How well did you copy these words?

Week 2 — Day 2

Copy out the labels on the plant. Then copy out the facts below.

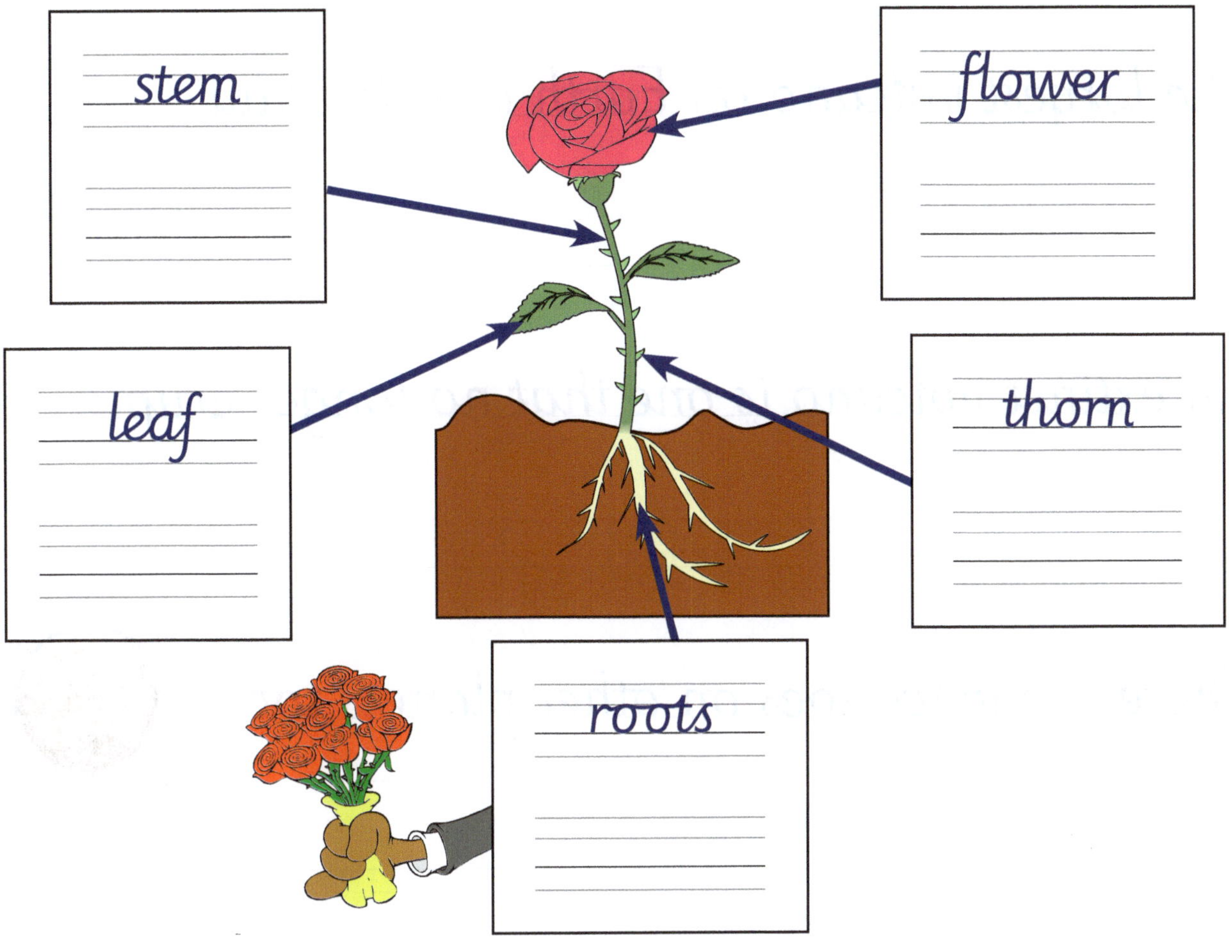

stem

flower

leaf

thorn

roots

The thorns on roses protect them from being eaten.

The oldest rosebush is over 1000 years old.

How did you get on with this page?

Week 2 — Day 3

Here are some facts about volcanoes. Copy each one out underneath.

The largest volcano on Earth is in Hawaii.

An extinct volcano is one that no longer erupts.

There are volcanoes on other planets too.

A volcanologist is a person who studies volcanoes.

Some volcanoes are underwater.

How neatly did you write these facts?

Week 2 — Day 4

These are instructions for making your own mini volcano. Copy out each step on the lines below.

Put a plastic bottle inside a cardboard cone.

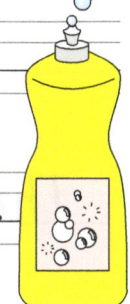

Mix bicarbonate of soda and washing up liquid.

Pour this into the bottle, along with some water.

Then add red food colouring and vinegar.

Watch your volcano erupt!

How did you find copying these instructions?

Week 2 — Day 5

Here is some information about the Egyptian god, Thoth. Copy the sentences out in the spaces below.

The Ancient Egyptians believed in many gods.

Thoth was the oldest and wisest of them all.

Thoth was linked to writing and science.

He had the head of an ibis, which is a type of bird.

He was the god of scribes (people who wrote).

How did you get on with copying these sentences?

Week 3 — Day 1

Copy out each of these words twice.
Be as neat as you can.

reign

learn

consider

arrive

describe

particular

through

occasion

occasionally

knowledge

How neatly did you copy these words?

Week 3 — Day 2

Here are some plural nouns. You use a plural when there is more than one of something. Copy each word out twice.

balloons

earthquakes

paintbrushes

superheroes

 babies

families

loaves

geese

children

snowmen

How did you get on with these plural nouns?

Week 3 — Day 3

These phrases all use apostrophes to show that the second thing belongs to the first thing. Copy each phrase out once on the lines below.

the fish's umbrella   Levi's cookies

Nigel's bath time   a dog's dinner

Chloe's messy bedroom   Grandma's house

Meena's favourite multicoloured trainers

the unicorn's horn   the firefighter's gold medal

How did you do with these phrases?

Week 3 — Day 4

These sentences are all about ways to stay healthy. Copy each one out on the lines below.

Eat at least five portions of fruit and veg a day.

Make sure you drink plenty of water every day.

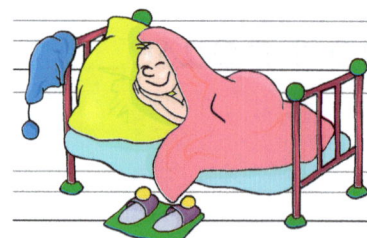

Always try to get a good night's sleep.

Walk to school if you can, or ride your bike.

Don't forget to brush your teeth twice a day!

How healthy is your handwriting looking today?

Year 3 Handwriting — Spring Term

Week 3 — Day 5

Here are Kim's instructions for a fitness routine.
Copy them out carefully below.

1. Stretch your arms up high above your head.

2. Bend down and touch your toes.

3. Do 10 star jumps as quickly as you can.

4. Run up and down on the spot for 30 seconds.

5. Balance on one leg for 20 seconds.

How did you get on with these instructions?

Week 4 — Day 1

Write each of these words out three times. Be as neat as you can.

complete

library

strange

possible

ordinary

different

grammar

guide

naughty

February

How did you get on with these words?

Week 4 — Day 2

Copy these adjectives and comparison words once.
Can you join up the pairs too? One has already been done for you.

small	angrier
slow	prettiest
cute	funnier
greedy	slowest
tall	cleverer
pretty	smallest
clever	younger
funny	cutest
angry	taller
young	greedier

How do you think this page went?

Week 4 — Day 3

These sentences use words that compare things and people. Copy each one out underneath.

I am shorter than my dad.

Your pet rabbit is the fluffiest.

I think yellow flowers are the prettiest.

My brother is the fastest runner at school.

This recipe is trickier than that one.

How did this page go?

Week 4 — Day 4

You might use these phrases when you write a postcard. Copy them out below.

Dear Uncle Steven,   How are you?

We had a lovely day.   What did you do?

Larissa went swimming in the sea.

Mum's shoes got very sandy.   I miss you!

Take care!   Love from, Cara

Could you write each of these phrases neatly?

Week 4 — Day 5

This is a letter to your friend. Copy each line out. Can you write your name at the end?

Dear Alys,

Thank you for coming to my party.

What have you been doing this week?

I have been eating lots of yummy cake today!

Tomorrow, we are going to a concert.

Lots of love from,

How did you find writing this letter?

Week 5 — Day 1

These words only use short letters. Copy them out three times.
Try to make all of the letters the same size.

mirror

armour

corner

version

camera

summer

cream

worse

museum

mission

serious

mouse

How did you find writing on a single line?

Week 5 — Day 2

These words include some tall letters. Copy them three times.
Try to make all the tall letters (except 't') the same height.

sailor

anchor

boat

climb

bucket

kettle

beach

launch

double

handle

knock

turtle

Did you write these words neatly?

Week 5 — Day 3

 Each of these words includes letters with tails. Practise making the tails the same length. Copy each word out three times.

finger

jaguar

snipping

pyjamas

quarry

puppy

creepy

spying

sponge

 enjoy

jumping

spring

Were your tails all the same length on this page?

Week 5 — Day 4

Here are six sentences for you to copy out underneath. Make sure your capital letters are the same height as your tall letters.

The sheep played chess against Arvid.

I went to visit my friend, Finlay, in Edinburgh.

Kateri was the best cowgirl in Edmonton.

There are lots of penguins in Antarctica.

Tina and Pasha met up in Brighton for a coffee.

Paris is the capital city of France.

How did you get on with these sentences?

Week 5 — Day 5

This is a story about going to the beach. Copy each line out below it.

Yesterday, my family had a barbecue on the beach.

My dad dropped his burger in the sand!

After I ate mine, I built a sandcastle.

Then Ross and I decided to go surfing,

but I fell off my surfboard and got very wet.

So we sat in the sun and had an ice cream.

How did you find this page?

Week 6 — Day 1

Copy out each of these words three times. Try your best to make each letter the correct height. Look out for tall letters and letters with tails.

increase

mention

notice

popular

regular

though

although

special

length

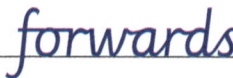

forwards

question

purpose

How did you get on with these words?

Week 6 — Day 2

Conjunctions are used to join words and phrases together. Copy each of these conjunctions out three times.

or

and

but

since

yet

although

while

until

because

when

before

after

Did you copy these conjunctions neatly?

Week 6 — Day 3

Copy each of these sentences out neatly on the line below.
Can you spot the conjunction in each one?

I'll be quiet now since you've stopped listening.

He wants ice skates, but they're expensive.

It's raining, so the match is cancelled.

They went for a walk before they had lunch.

I like doing jigsaws and making bread.

She cycled every day until her bike was stolen.

Did you manage to copy these sentences neatly?

Week 6 — Day 4

There are some unusual excuses below.
Copy each one out underneath.

I didn't wash up because the Prime Minister called.

 *I did my homework, but my fish ate it.*

I was falsely arrested, so I didn't tidy my room.

I couldn't go because I had to rescue a penguin.

The vase broke because I threw it at a burglar.

I didn't practise this week because I lost my piano.

How did you get on with copying these excuses?

Week 6 — Day 5

These are some instructions for a treasure hunt. Copy them out below.

1. Start at the north entrance to the clock tower.

2. Walk north until you reach the big ash tree.

3. Turn left and follow the winding stone path.

4. When you get to the river, cross the bridge.

5. Walk east until you reach a fence.

6. Find the brass fence post and dig for the treasure!

Could you copy these instructions neatly?

Week 7 — Day 1

Copy out each of these words three times.

century

promise

eighth

caught

exercise

experiment

strength

busy

business

famous

straight

important

How did you get on with these words?

Week 7 — Day 2

> Adverbs describe how something is done. They often end in '-ly'. Here are some examples. Copy each adverb out three times.

kindly

quickly

loudly

anxiously

lightly

gracefully

wisely

angrily

sneakily

tightly

sweetly

superbly

How neatly did you write these adverbs?

Week 7 — Day 3

Copy out each of the sentences below. Can you spot the adverbs?

The crowd watched the match noisily.

He hoped that he'd get a lolly if he asked nicely.

The mouse speedily scurried out of sight.

She proudly showed her medal to her parents.

They stared hungrily at the blueberry muffins.

 I waited nervously for my turn on the stage.

How did you do with these sentences?

Week 7 — Day 4

 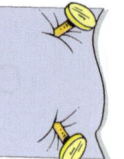

Here are six sentences that all contain adverbs. Copy each one once.

He rudely interrupted the man's speech.

The knight bravely fought the dragon.

She thought sadly about the necklace she had lost.

The class was silently listening to the teacher.

The spaniel wagged her tail cheerfully.

I gratefully accepted the first prize.

How did you find copying these sentences?

Week 7 — Day 5

Here is a recipe for a banana split.
Copy the recipe out in the space underneath.

1. Carefully cut a peeled banana down the middle.

2. Place the banana halves into a bowl.

3. Put two scoops of ice cream on the bananas.

4. Squirt some cream and chocolate sauce on top.

5. Add any other toppings you like, such as strawberry sauce, nuts or a cherry.

How neat is your recipe looking?

Week 8 — Day 1

Copy each of these words out three times. Try to make the tails of the letters 'p', 'g' and 'y' the same length.

bicycle

potatoes

experience

height

sentence

opposite

suppose

actual

pressure

possess

actually

possession

How did you find this page?

Week 8 — Day 2

Prepositions tell you where something is or when something happens. Copy each preposition three times.

on

below

until

before

over

with

through

into

after

while

above

inside

How did you get on with these prepositions?

Week 8 — Day 3

This is a story about space. Copy each sentence out below. Can you spot the prepositions?

A rocket flew around the Sun and out into space.

The rocket landed on a planet.

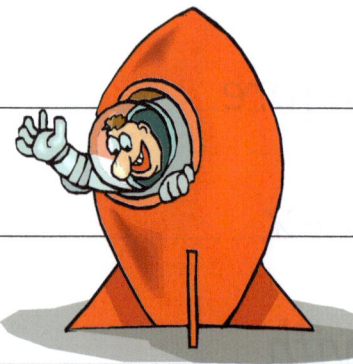

Outside the rocket was an alien.

The alien was standing next to her spaceship.

The alien jumped into her spaceship

and flew past the rocket.

How did you find these sentences?

Week 8 — Day 4

Practise writing these sentences as neatly as you can.

Sheetal is practising her song before the show.

Marc performed in front of the audience.

Phoebe danced with Jakob until midnight.

The director worked behind the scenes.

A dog jumped through a hoop on the stage.

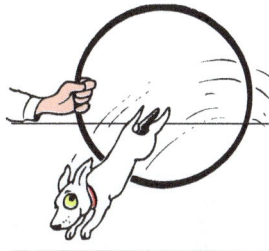

I sat in the audience during the play.

How neatly did you copy out this page?

Week 8 — Day 5

Here is a poem for you to copy out. It contains lots of prepositions. Write each line in the space on the right.

Beneath the umbrella,

inside my old raincoat,

next to the window,

on the wet pavement,

in my green wellies.

Into the sweetshop,

past the counter,

among the glass jars,

beyond the pear drops,

to the best sweet of all.

How did you find writing out this poem?

Week 9 — Day 1

Copy each of these words out three times.
Try to make sure every letter is the right size.

weight

medicine

calendar

probably

address

quarter

heard

breath

breathe

heart

build

answer

How neatly did you write these words?

Week 9 — Day 2

Each of the words on the left rhymes with one of the words on the right. Copy out each word underneath. Then see if you can draw lines to connect the words that rhyme. One has been done for you.

wishes — cashew

spill   slight

eye   dishes

flew   quill

kite   high

style   while

How did you get on with this page?

Week 9 — Day 3

Here are some rhyming couplets.
Copy out each pair of lines in the space below.

Last night I had an amazing dream.

I was playing football for my favourite team.

I want to be in a rock band as a drummer.

We'll play at festivals every summer.

I want a big pond full of newts and frogs.

I think they're more fun than cats and dogs.

How do you think you did with these couplets?

Week 9 — Day 4

This is a poem by Edward Lear. Copy out each line underneath. Your exclamation marks should be the same height as your tall letters.

There was an Old Man with a beard,

 Who said, "It is just as I feared!—

Two Owls and a Hen,

 Four Larks and a Wren,

Have all built their nests in my beard!"

How did you get on with this poem?

Week 9 — Day 5

This is the second verse from the poem 'Jabberwocky' by Lewis Carroll. It's got a lot of nonsense words in it. Copy it out as neatly as you can.

"Beware the Jabberwock, my son!

The jaws that bite, the claws that catch!

Beware the Jubjub bird, and shun

The frumious Bandersnatch!"

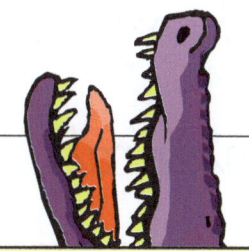

How neatly do you think you copied this verse?

Week 10 — Day 1

> Copy each of these words out three times.
> Make each word as neat as you can.

extreme

earth

enough

interest

material

minute

fruit

group

decide

forwards

therefore

natural

How did you get on with these words?

Week 10 — Day 2

Here are two word families. The top five words are related to 'place' and the bottom five are related to 'sign'. Copy each word three times.

place

replace

misplace

placement

displace

sign

signal

signify

significant

signature

How did you find this page?

Week 10 — Day 3

This page is full of facts about Boudica. Copy each line out underneath. Make sure all your capital letters are the same height.

Boudica was the queen of a Celtic tribe.

When the king died, the Romans took her land.

She led a massive rebellion against them.

The rebels set fire to cities and killed many people.

Eventually, the Romans won the battles,

but Boudica is still known as a hero.

How did this page about Boudica go?

Week 10 — Day 4

Copy out each of these lines below.
Can you tell which fairy tale each one is about?

Her carriage turned into a pumpkin at midnight.

His nose got longer whenever he lied.

They left a trail of breadcrumbs in the wood.

The prince climbed up her long, golden hair.

The wolf dressed up as her grandmother.

He traded his cow for some magic beans.

How neatly did you write each sentence?

Week 10 — Day 5

Here is an ancient Greek myth for you to copy out. Copy it out in the space below. Be as neat as you can.

King Midas was granted one wish by a Greek god. Midas wished that all the things he touched turned to gold. But all his food turned to gold, then his daughter turned to gold. So Midas begged the gods to undo the curse. After that, he stopped being greedy.

How did you find copying out this myth?

Week 11 — Day 1

Here is a list of words. Copy each one out three times.

believe

various

accident

often

thought

remember

centre

exercise

strength

caught

surprise

difficult

How neatly do you think you wrote these words?

Week 11 — Day 2

Here are two word families. Copy each word out three times. Can you see the word which links each family?

cover

covering

discover

recovered

 bedcover

act

actor

 activate

actively

counteract

How neatly did you copy these words?

Week 11 — Day 3

These sentences all contain words that you can use instead of 'said'. Copy each sentence out below.

"Stop!" she yelled at the top of her lungs.

The ghost whispered its secret.

"There's a fly in my soup!" he complained.

My mum called my name from downstairs.

The teacher announced that he's leaving the school.

"You can't sing," my brother sneered.

Would you say you've done well with this page?

Week 11 — Day 4

These sentences all use inverted commas to show which words are being spoken. Copy each one out underneath.

"Hey! Stop that!" Mr Nichols shouted.

_____

"I think I've found the treasure!" cried the Captain.

_____

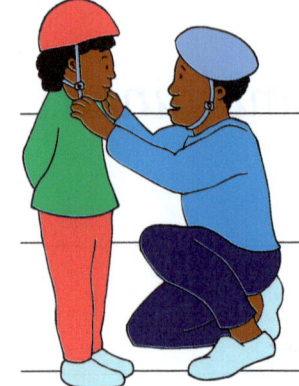

"Did you post that letter?" asked Mum.

_____

"You never forget how to ride a bike."

_____

"I really can't find Morris anywhere."

_____

"You've fractured this bone," the doctor explained.

_____

How well do you think you did with this page?

Week 11 — Day 5

Here is the beginning of a story. Copy it out in the space underneath.

"A parcel has arrived with your names on it," said Mrs Sangha. She passed it to her daughters. Asha tore it open excitedly. "Wow," she gasped. It was a huge orange gemstone. "Why has someone sent us this?" asked Samrita. "Wait!" Asha declared. "There's a note…"

How neatly did you copy this paragraph?

Week 12 — Day 1

Here are twelve words for you to copy out.
Write each one three times.

island

peculiar

eight

imagine

length

promise

favourite

perhaps

disappear

continue

special

 appear

How well did you write these words?

Week 12 — Day 2

The verbs on the left are in the present tense. The verbs on the right are in the past tense. Copy each word once.

dive	dived
go	went
look	looked
swim	swam
jump	jumped
eat	ate
talk	talked
paddle	paddled
move	moved
catch	caught
splash	splashed
walk	walked

How did you find writing these verbs?

Week 12 — Day 3

Each of these sentences is in the past tense. Copy them out underneath.

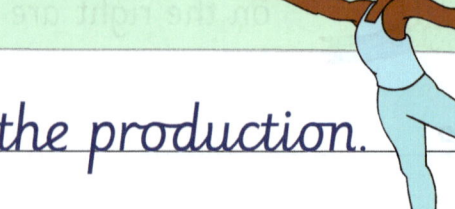

Will danced the lead role in the production.

She played for the best football team in the league.

Melissa skated after the ice hockey puck.

Sarah went to the cinema last night.

Syed drank a large glass of milk before breakfast.

I climbed a tall mountain with my friends.

How neatly did you write these sentences?

Week 12 — Day 4

These sentences are all about a camping trip. They are written in the present perfect tense. Copy each one out below.

We have all gone camping together.

Mum has cooked some sausages over the fire.

I have toasted lots of marshmallows.

My sister has put up our tents.

Dad has spent all day fishing.

Now everyone else has fallen asleep.

How do you think this page went?

Week 12 — Day 5

Here is some information about how people lived in the Iron Age. Copy it out at the bottom of the page.

In the Iron Age, people often lived in hillforts. They built large walls around the tops of hills, and they lived and farmed inside them. The walls, made of earth or wood, protected them from other tribes who tried to steal their animals. They also built roundhouses made of wood and mud.

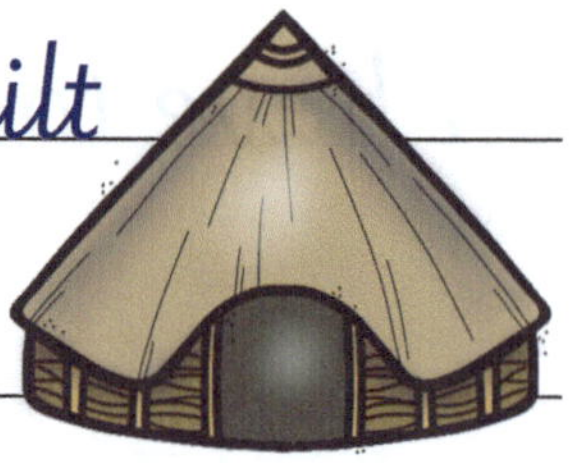

How neat do you think your writing is?